Mental

Toughness

The Extreme Guide to Build an Unbeatable,

Strong and Resilience Mind, With the

Leadership's Mindset.

The Training for Success Like a Navy Seals.

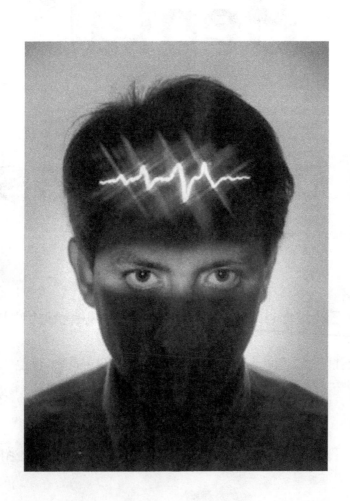

Table of Contents

Additionally, the information in the following pages is intended only for informational purposes and should thus be thought of as universal. As befitting its nature, it is presented without assurance regarding its prolonged validity or interim quality. Trademarks that are mentioned are done without written consent and can in no way be considered an endorsement from the trademark holder.

Introduction

Congratulations on downloading *Mental Toughness* and thank you for doing so.

The following chapters will discuss exactly what is mental toughness, how you can achieve and improve your mental toughness, the benefits of having mental toughness, traits and characteristics of a person who has mental toughness. You will also discover how fear and stress interact with mental toughness and how developing your mental toughness can help you deal with these two issues. You will also learn more about setting goals and how mental toughness can help you achieve these goals more effectively and efficiently.

Furthermore, you will learn a great deal about emotional intelligence, including what emotional intelligence is, and when and how to use it. There are many ways in which having a higher level of emotional intelligence can benefit you. You will learn how to develop and use these skills by reading this book, so that by the end it, you will have a comprehensive understanding of what emotional intelligence is and how to hone and utilize these skills to improve your life. There are plenty of books on this subject on the market, thanks again for choosing this one! Every effort was made to ensure it is full of as much useful information as possible. Please enjoy!

Chapter 1: What is Mental Toughness?

Mental toughness may mean something different to you than it means to someone else. Oftentimes, people think about surmounting hurdles and challenges that present themselves in order to keep pushing forward toward a goal. But what allows a person to form the drive and motivation to desire and believe that he can achieve that goal, and then to formulate a plan to achieve that goal? What gets the person to stop procrastinating and take steps toward achieving that goal? And what allows the person to stay focused, not get frustrated, not give up and follow through on trying to achieve that goal until he actually achieves it? Mental toughness is what it takes to channel your motivation, determination, and desire to achieve the objective you've set.

It takes mental toughness to be on your way to achieving your goals and to take all of the steps that are listed above without getting sidetracked by distractions, emotions, thoughts, and other things that can take you off of your path.

In fact, everything that a person wants to achieve in life takes some degree of mental toughness. How much mental toughness it takes is based on the difficulty of the goal. This is especially true because things may not always be easy for you to do and your goals may not be easy to accomplish. Learning how to develop your mental toughness can help you tremendously when setting out to achieve your goal. In fact, it is so important that you have a significant degree of mental toughness when trying to achieve the goals that you have in life. Education, money, and connection may all come in second, third, and fourth to having the mental toughness and fortitude to establish your goal, stick to it, and believe that you can achieve it.

Mental toughness is often thought of as resilience - the ability to withstand what life throws at you and to keep going. One example of this comes into play when discussing mental toughness and professional athletics. If a major league baseball pitcher walks three batters in a row, he still must have the resilience to stand on the mound and pitch to the next batter even though the crowd might be booing, the backup pitcher may be warming up, the coach may be yelling at him, and his teammates are disappointed.

Why Do You Need Mental Toughness?

Mental toughness is required to manage emotions.
Mental toughness is required to control and handle your thoughts.
Mental toughness is the key to willpower.
Mental toughness is required to navigate through trying times. *Mental toughness is required for everyday life situations.*

Why Do You Need Mental Toughness?

Your mental state is just as important, if not more important, than the amount of knowledge, skill or money you have when you are trying to achieve a goal. There are a lot of people out there with the knowledge and education that they need to accomplish big dreams, but they do not have the proper mental state to do so. They may state moving along the way toward a goal and then back down for fear that they may fail, it will take too long, be too difficult, or somehow has otherwise become impossible. In fact, many people fail to state on their way toward achieving big goals at all because either they do not believe that it can be done, or they do not have the strength of mind to think that they can do it.

Mental toughness can provide you the inner strength that you need to be on your way to achieving your goals. Much of a person's inner strength to persevere and achieve is derived from his or her mental state. Thus, it is important for you to have a strong, stable mental state in which you can think clearly and, understand your emotions and desires, and take active steps toward achieving your goals.

Mental toughness is required to manage emotions.

It is unavoidable that people will experience emotions. Emotions are a naturally occurring state of mind that is the result of a person's surrounds, mood, and relationships and interactions with other people. Because emotions are naturally occurring, they may actually overtake a person's thoughts and become their main focus if a person lets them do so. This is where mental toughness comes in. Mental toughness gives a person the ability to control, to some extent, his or her emotions, as well as the way in which he or she reacts to them and how much these emotions take over the person's mind.

For instance, you may have had a fight with your spouse or significant other in the morning which has you stressed out, sad or feeling some other emotion that is not conducive to getting a great deal of work done. Some people may not get much accomplished that day or even irritate their co-workers or make mistakes on the job because they are focusing on their emotions. A person who has mastered mental toughness, however, should be able to perform at a high level even if he or she still cares about the argument and has experienced some of the same emotions as the person who messes up at work that day. The saying 'it's not what happens to you, it's how you handle it' is true to a significant extent.

Thus, mental toughness is very important when you seek to handle your emotions properly so that you can make wise and effective decisions while still experiencing emotions.

Mental toughness is required to control and handle your thoughts.

Thoughts differ from emotions due to the fact that they are not always about feelings. In fact, a significant portion of our time is spent thinking about things that do not have much to do with our emotions. You may think about whether or not you are going to be able to finish your homework or work project on time. Although the thought of not finishing the assignment on time may evoke some feelings and emotions, the thought of whether or not you will finish the assignment on time is not primarily based on emotion.

In order to think clearly and focus, you need to be able to control your thought. However, a challenge arises when there is a lot of things that are going on around you, and you find it difficult to focus on or even identify what is and what is not important. This is why it is so important to have mental toughness. Mental toughness can help you to control your thought processes so that you can focus and concentrate on the things that you need to be focused on or the task at hand despite whatever is going on in the world around you.

There are some key people who are known to need and have an exceptional level of mental toughness. People such as performer and world-class athletes must possess a tremendous amount of mental toughness to perform in front of millions of people and excel without getting distracted by the crowd noise, problems at home, worries that they have and more. Examples of people who possess this type of mental toughness include people such as Beyoncé, NFL players, Tiger Woods, and more. Beyoncé must get up on stage and perform for crowds of thousands of people on the day of the concert whether she is feeling happy, sad, sick or tired. She must remain focused to hit her dance steps perfectly, remember her songs even with the crowd noise and some of the fans singing along.

Furthermore, the amount of talent that she has would not get her to where she is alone. She had to have the drive to get to the top, and she had to be determined along the way and stay focused. There are a lot of other singing acts and groups that were around when she started that were considered to be just as good as Destiny's Child from which she came. Many of these groups and the singers in them are no longer around because they did not have the mental toughness to forge along through all of the struggles and hurdles that it takes to get to the top of the music field.

In fact, many people may not even want to be where Beyoncé is because they understand that it is too much mental pressure for them to handle. Many people would like to accomplish much smaller goals with far fewer people watching in order to minimize the mental pressure that is put upon them. This is why most of the articles and books that you find about mental toughness are focused on professional athletes and major performers, so much so that they often neglect giving advice to the average layman about how he can utilize mental toughness in his daily life. Throughout this book, however, you will learn how to develop mental toughness even if you never plan to play a professional sport or get up on a stage and perform for a crowd of millions because everyone can benefit from developing and increasing their mental toughness to that they can move to new heights in their own lives.

Just think about how much mental toughness a major league baseball player must have to stand at the plate with a baseball being thrown in his direction so close to him at almost 100 miles an hour if not more. He must be able to block out the crowd and not let the number of people who are watching cloud his judgment in any way. This is not an easy feat to accomplish, but it is a necessary one is he is to have any chance of succeeding at the game.

Mental toughness is the key to willpower. Most people would be surprised to find out that willpower or lack thereof is the primary obstacle that most people face when trying to better themselves. You would probably assume that it would be money, race or class; however, in this day and age, it is possible to achieve almost anything that you want in spite of these obstacles which used to limit people in the past but are no longer considered to be hurdles today. The lack of the ability to stick to something and see it through and have the determination to make it to a set target is the obstacle that people face. This is something that is within your control; therefore, a lot of people think that they can make a few small adjustments and they will have the willpower and the determination that they need to accomplish something that they want to do. They soon find out that they were wrong when they thought that gaining willpower meant a few small changes and they were on their way toward the end goal that they desired. No, willpower takes *a lot* of major changes and hard work. The main thing that you need to change to gain more willpower is your mind. Mental toughness plays a substantial role in willpower as willpower is considered to be one of the key traits that those who have mental toughness display.

Mental toughness is required to navigate through trying times.

During times when you are doing well, have some money in the bank, your relationships are good, you are in good health, and you are rather happy, mental toughness may not be called in as much unless it is I certain high-pressure situations. However; if you ever experience hard times such as the death of a spouse or a child, loss of a job and source of income, a natural disaster or something of that nature, it is very important for you to have mental toughness to get through the situation that you are in the best that you can and get back on your feet. Hard times really are a test of your will. And hard times can happen to anybody whether they expect it and have planned for it or not.

To be prepared for whatever life throws at you and prepared for a hard time should you experience them, it is good to develop some mental toughness skills in advance. In fact, if you have never experienced true hard times, things that would not seem like as big a deal to someone who has may seem like a bigger deal to you. Thus, you will feel that you need some mental toughness to navigate through life and succeed.

Wrestling with Mental Toughness

Mental toughness is required for everyday life situations. Suppose you are driving your care, the same car that you had for the last four years, down a road and you swerve to avoid hitting a deer than just ran into the street and run off of the road. As your car is careening toward a group of trees whether you go into full panic mode and let fate take over or you attempt to steer depends on how much mental toughness you have. I experienced a similar situation, and the main thing that I found out is that a group of trees looks much denser from the road; however, the trees are far enough apart that you can steer through them if you have the wherewithal to do so. A friend of mine was a passenger in a car in which a car accident was about to occur. Instead of trying to help the driver concentrate on steering, she suggested that we all pray together (The driver ignored her suggesting and used navigation skills instead of prayer to avoid the accident). If my friend in the driver's seat had been the driver when my car ran off the road, I do not

believe that she would have made it because she may

have been to in shock to realize that steering and

maneuvering through the trees somewhat is possible.

One of the reasons that my friend may not have survived if she had been in the first car accident is that she does not possess the same amount of mental toughness that I have conditioned myself to utilize, especially in tough and trying situations. I would say she lacks a substantial amount of mental toughness; however, some people may disagree and argue that she possesses a normal amount of mental toughness. This is a skill she may never have tried to hone. But then you can look at the fact that she wanted to go to graduate school, but she didn't because she didn't believe that's he could get the money or would have the time. I, on the other hand, graduated from graduate school because I did not look for the hurdles to stop me, I looked for the hurdles to go.

In everyday life, situations that require mental toughness often present themselves and for you to get through the situation intact, you need to have already developed some mental toughness skills that will allow you to handle that specific situation. Therefore, it is wise for you to take some of the practice lessons in this book to heart and learn some skills for enhancing your mental toughness so that you can handle life at your best.

Chapter 2: Traits of the Unbeatable Mind

The unbeatable mind is strong and tough. It is resilient and relentless. It is determined, and it has the willpower and the drive to succeed. We all want an unbeatable mind and often get frustrated when we fall short of what we wanted to accomplish because we just could not stay focused and determined. Focus and determination are both products of having mental strength. These are some of the traits that the unbeatable mind people possess.

There are certain traits or characteristics that a person must possess in order to develop and establish mental toughness. Some of these traits are some important that if you do not possess them, you may need to take the time to develop these traits before you can hope to gain mental toughness.

Traits of the Unbeatable Mind

1) Mental Competency
2) Emotional Intelligence
3) Resilience
4) Willpower
5) A Winner's Mind
6) The Ability to Focus
7) They Surround Themselves with Other People Who Are Mentally Tough
8) They Avoid Trying Too Hard to Go Against the Grain
9) Expect Delayed Gratification
10) Consistency, Consistency, Consistency

Trait 1: Mental Competency

The first trait that you must possess to develop and sustain a certain level of mental toughness is mental competency. Having a sound and competent mind is the very first thing that you need to gain mental toughness. Mental competency is the ability to make sound judgement decisions. Thus, it is important to pay attention to and take care of your mental health before developing your mental competence. Taking care of your mental health is important to having the proper foundational environment for mental toughness to develop. Disorders such as bipolar disorder can cloud your judgement and make it very difficult for you to develop mental toughness.

Don't assume that your mental health and mental competency does not change when certain things in your life change. If you experience something such as a death or a severe emotional loss or you are going through post-partum depression, or you just entered menopause, take the time to go get your mental health checked out. This is a very important step to developing an unbeatable mind.

Trait 2: Emotional Intelligence

Emotional intelligence can be characterized as a type of emotional competency, similar to mental competency for the emotions. Emotional competency is the ability to identify, understand and control your own emotions while being able to identify and understand the emotions of others and adjust properly to these emotions.

Having a low level of emotional intelligence can make it very hard to succeed in areas of life that involve other people. For instance, a person who lacks emotional intelligence may find it hard to succeed in relationships due to the fact that he cannot identify and understand the emotions of potential dates and mates. This may lead to a significant amount of communication issues, a lack of enjoyment in the relationship, and the inability to form relationships altogether.

Moreover, having a low level of self-awareness can cause you to identify your own emotions improperly. You may fail to realize how you truly feel about a person, job, or issue because you were not in touch with your emotions. This can lead to less satisfaction in these areas of your life. A high level of emotional intelligence leads to self-awareness. A person who has mastered emotional intelligence skills is more likely to do things that lead to a higher level of satisfaction for him or her because he or she knows himself better.

People who excel in the area of emotional intelligence, however, may find it very easy to deal with people and gravitate toward people. The reason that these people tend to gravitate toward other people is that people have a tendency to reach to them well. There are two key factors which have a significant impact on the way in which people react to them, and these are 1) empathy and 2) and increased ability to communicate with others.

Empathy is the ability to understand the thoughts and feelings of another person. It is the ability to put yourself in their shoes so to speak. People who can empathize with others are more likely to make other people comfortable around them and feel relaxed. Furthermore, people tend to feel that the empathetic person cares more about their day or how they are doing than people who have not developed the skill to emphasize with others. This can lead to deeper connections. Thus, a person who has emotional intelligence and can emphasize with others is more like to have more positive strong connections with people than a person who does not know how to emphasize with others. And these strong connections are a support system upon which a person can build more mental toughness.

A person with emotional intelligence has better communication skills. Being able to understand other people's emotions and adjust accordingly aids in conversation skills tremendously. Understanding the emotions of others can keep you from saying things which are off-putting or offensive, both thing that can quickly end a conversation and convince the other person not to communicate as much with you in the future.

Communication skills are derived from not only having the ability to understand emotions and speech; it includes reading and understanding the use of body language, personalities and more. Much of communication is about listening. To be a good listener, you should learn to listen actively. Do not just stand there passively as a conversation is taking place, that a strong interest in the words that are being said. And be sure that you notice the facial expression and the body language. Hand gestures are also good for you to notice. Take in the whole scene and make a judgement with that in mind.

Trait 3: Resilience

Resilience is the cornerstone trait of mental toughness. In fact, many people consider resilience to be the definition of mental toughness. Resilience is the ability to persevere and persist even though the challenges that life brings you. It is the ability to dust yourself off after a setback and get back up and try again and again until you succeed. Resilience is what helps people to overcome the challenges and obstacles that they find when they start trying to achieve a certain goal.

There are a number of factors that make up resilience. One of the factors that play a role in resilience is possessing confidence in yourself. You must have confidence in order to succeed. Confidence is the belief that you can accomplish the goal that you have set out to accomplish, that you are good enough, and you deserve to achieve your goal. To achieve a lofty goal, you have to believe that you can.

Therefore, confidence is also the ability to limit and control your negative beliefs in yourself so that they do not outweigh the positive ones that are telling you that you can succeed. Throughout life, many people have formed a significant amount of negative beliefs about whether or not they can be something that they want to be or do something that they want to do. People may have been led to believe that they are limited by where they are from, how much money they have, their skin color, their looks and more. These beliefs tend to reside in the back of people's minds and stop them from believing that they can achieve certain goals in life and that they need to 'stay in their place' and dream they type of dreams that were made for someone like them. Peers, teachers, classmates and more may have discouraged a person from trying to achieve certain goals instead of encouraging the person to go after them. Therefore, resilience is the ability to get past these negative affirmations that have been placed in our minds, sometimes over the span of years, and to reprogram ourselves to see our chances of achieving these goals in a more positive manner.

Trait 4: Willpower

People who are mentally tough have a significant amount of willpower. Willpower is the determination that is needed to do things such as lose 50 pounds, stop smoking, stick to an exercise routine and many other things in life.

Willpower is the ability to not give in to your negative desires. It is the ability to resist temptation in order to make changes in your life that will improve your life from its current state. In fact, a survey conducted by the American Psychological Association, it was found that the number 1 barrier that most people cited to making positive changes in their lives was the lack of willpower. Therefore, the most limiting factor that people face, according to the American Psychological Association is not the lack of money, lack of education, or the lack of time, it is the lack of the ability to resist negative temptation.

Willpower or lack thereof is one of the biggest hurdles that most people face. In order to quit smoking, you need to be able to withstand the urge to do so; but, the majority of people who try to quit smoking fail because their desire to quit is not as strong as their desire to smoke one more cigarette. Even though smokers who want to quit may be aware of all of the negative effects that smoking can have has on them such as a wide variety of health problems, high cost, stained teeth, walls and more, people still lack the sheer determination to quit the habit. A person who has mental toughness, however, is able to channel this determination and use it to effectively quit smoking. And willpower is the key to success in most of the goals that you have in life.

Trait 5: A Winner's Mind

Mentally tough people have the right mindset to achieve the task that they set out to achieve. They believe that they can do it and have a positive attitude and the likelihood that they will succeed. Having a winner's mind is about having the drive to push forward and not allowing yourself to take no for an answer. People with a winner's mind do have the willpower that is necessary to achieve the goals and dreams; in fact, this is something that many people with a winner's mind never even bother to call into question, unlike the rest of us.

Certain aspects are present within the winner's mind. A winner's mind is grateful for the things that he or she has. Being thankful for the things that you have allows you to have a positive attitude despite the things that you lack. A winner is glad for the everyday things that he or she was blessed with that will allow him or her to achieve his or her goals in life.

A winner's mind thinks positive thoughts. There are many people who allow their minds to be clogged with negative thoughts. This is something that is detrimental to their spirit, their mindset, and their likelihood of achieving the goals that they set out to accomplish. Winners concentrate on seeing things in a positive manner. In fact, winners try to surround themselves with a positive vibe and group of people altogether so that their mindset is connected to positivity.

In addition, a winner's mind is always ready and open to learn more and enhance the skills that the person possesses. Winners are constantly learning and developing and evolving in order to stay on top of their game.

Winners are always setting new goals. Once you reach one goal in life, a winner would not be satisfied to just sit back and be content that he or she had achieved that particular goal. Winner's tend to set new goals immediately after achieving one goal; the success of fulfilling one the first goal offers encouragement and confidence that the next goal that is set can be achieved as well. Winners also tend to set these goals in progression, or series, one right after the other, knocking them off like a to-do list. This helps to keep you motivated and striving to achieve more and more.

Trait 6: The Ability to Focus

We've all seen people who do not have a strong ability to focus and are easily distracted. In fact, there is a good chance that you are one of these people if you have not taken the time to try to develop your mental toughness. Mental strength improves your concentration. A significant number of exercises that are designed to help you improve your mental strength are focused on concentration.

Many high-performance athletes have tunnel vision when in their athletic performance mode so that they have a total and complete concentration that allows them to excel. This focus is necessary to make split-second decisions on how to deal with other players in order to come out on top. Many people who have never participated in these types of activities do not understand the type of focused zone these athletes get into and may have never honed their skills to get to total focus on the play at hand.

Trait 7: They Surround Themselves with Other People Who Are Mentally Tough

People with mental toughness tend to surround themselves with other people who are mentally tough. You often find that athletes and entertainers of a certain level tend to associate with each other, and you may have assumed that it is because they are celebrities or because they are highly paid. You may not realize that their work ethic may be part of the reason that they gravitate towards each other. Their careers are so demanding that other people may not understand this and may not agree with doing the same amount of work that they are willing to put in. These high-level performers keep each other on their toes and encourage each other.

And these people all possess a high degree of mental toughness which tends to feed off of each other. They can encourage each other to stay strong and work hard. They illustrate what mental toughness is in a given situation; they support each other and more.

It is rare that you see a person who seems to be strong mentally and emotionally closely associated with someone who is significantly weaker in these two categories. This is because, although the stronger one may rub off on and have an effect on the weaker one, the weaker one has an effect on the stronger one as well. The stronger one is being pulled down, and the weaker one is being pulled up toward a common average strength. This is often uncomfortable for both people. It can be frustrating for the stronger person who may often wonder why the weaker one fails to show as much willpower, determination, and drive, and it can be belittling for the weaker person who may experience insults and a condescending attitude from the other. Thus, it is beneficial for both people in associate more closely with someone on their level of mental strength.

This means that if you desire to develop your mental strength, you need to identify and surround yourself with people who possess mental strength as well. And you may have to eliminate or reduce association with some people who may keep you from reaching higher levels of mental strength.

Trait 8: They Avoid Trying Too Hard to Go Against the Grain

No, you should not always try to simply go with the flow and fit in. And the people known for having very high levels of emotional intelligence definitely stand out; however, there is nothing wrong with trying to fit in a little. Constantly trying to buck the system can get tiring and start to become frustrating.

In addition, this can place more stress and mental strain on a person. This takes up space in a person's minds and takes a good deal of his or her time that could have been spent on something else. Furthermore, trying to be different can start to take a toll on you emotionally. When working on improving emotional intelligence which is covered later in this book, you will learn to identify and understand other people's feelings and reactions and how to adjust to gain better responses from others.

Trait 9: Expect Delayed Gratification

People with mental strength do not need to reap immediate benefits for their work and actions. They are fine with the benefits coming in time for the work that they did and the time that they put in. Seeking instant gratification can keep you from achieving what you could have achieved if you understood that the payout for the work that you put in does not always come immediately. Sometimes, it may take years to see the fruits of your labor. It is still important to keep going in order to see the benefits of your work.

Honing your mental strength will allow you to see that rewards are not the only good thing that you receive from your hard labor. There is the pride of a job well done and accomplishing your goals. You can also enjoy helping others in some way. And the rewards for your hard labor will come in time.

Trait 10: Consistent, Consistent, Consistent

People with mental toughness are consistent. Consistency goes along with expecting delayed gratification and patience; however, it does differ slightly. As previously stated, one of the most notable times when we discuss mental strength is with professional athletics. It is very important for professional athletes to be able to perform consistently at a high level. When watching an NFL game, you often hear the quarterback being judged on his consistency. One great play or game is not enough; to be the starting quarterback whom the team builds their offense around and has kids wearing his jersey, he must be consistency through the plays of the game, game after game.

Consistency is not just important in sports; it is important in life in general. It is vital that a doctor in the operating room is consistent and that a trial lawyer is consistent with his results. Consistency is the ability to produce the same high- quality results over and over again. This is done by understanding what you did right and how you did it as well as what you did wrong and what you need to do to fix it. After you identify what you did right, make sure that you *study* your performance to understand exactly how you did it so that you can repeat it. If you did it differently from others and still got it right. Was it luck? Luck will not allow you to produce consistency. To be consistent, there must be a solid foundation based on knowledge skill, and practice as well as performance in real-world situations.

Try to understand where and why you differed. If your correct answer or means of doing something differed from the norm, examine where and how it differed and assess whether the normal way would be easier for *you* to perform. addition, you may want to examine which way is capable of being reproduced repeatedly.

To be consistent, one must practice, practice, practice, and learn, learn. You have to understand how things are done step by step in order to be consistent. This takes a more thorough interest in and understanding of what you are doing than having a few great performances.

Common Habits of People with Mental Toughness

Be Calm, Cool and Collected
Not Wasting Time Concentrating on Things You Cannot Control
Leave the Past in the Past but Learn from It
Change Yourself but Don't Try to Change Others
Don't Waste Time on Envy and Jealousy
Not Spending a Great Deal of Time Worrying About What Others Think About You
Be Thankful for Everything That You Have
Don't Criticize
Live in the Present, Not the Future

Common Habits of People with Mental Toughness

Be Calm, Cool and Collected

The first habit that people with mental toughness display that you should try to emulate is that of caring themselves as if they are cool, calm, collected and in control of every situation that they are in. And they do this, even if they are not completely sure that they can control the situation.

Acting and thinking as if you are leaving parts of a situation up to luck and prayer, although this may seem like it brings hope to many people, can cause you to feel that you are not in control of the situation and you are powerless to truly control what is going on around you and the situation that you are in.

Feeling and acting as if you are in control can give you an underlying mindset that you have control over the world around you. This mentality has a significant impact on the way that you think and behave.

Not Wasting Time Concentrating on Things You Cannot Control

In fact. Spending a significant amount of time and energy thinking about the things that are beyond your control or that you cannot change can be draining on your energy, frustrating, a waste of time, and a confidence killer. Similar to what they say in Alcoholics Anonymous, "You need to have the courage to accept that the things that you can change and change the things that you can and have the wisdom to know the difference." People with mental toughness tend to abide by this statement even if they have never been an alcoholic. Things that are beyond your control should also be beyond your focus.

No one is blessed with endless mental energy; therefore, one habit that people with mental toughness display is the ability to stop wasting their time thinking about the things that are out of their reach or control so that they can spend more time focusing on all of the things that they have full control over.

This differs from the aforementioned being calm, cool, and collected because you can actually be calm and cool while occupying your mind and your thoughts with activities and events that are not within your control. Stay focused on things that you do have control over.

Leave the Past in the Past but Learn from It

The past does have its place, but it is definitely in the past is what people who have mastered mental toughness definitely understand.

Yes, it is important to learn from the past so that you do not repeat the same mistakes. However, you should not be overly focused on or consumed by the past. This is true whether the past was good or bad.

It is easy to understand why you should not spend a great deal of time focused on the past if it was full of negative things. However, many people often fail to realize that it is equally harmful to spend your time focusing on the past it if was great. If you were a star running back in college but hold down a regular nine to five now, spending a great deal of time going over and trying to relive the heroic moments of your past can cause you to waste time and even miss out of the present. And it is the present that prepares you for the future.

You cannot live in or relive the past. It is over. Even if the memories and the lessons from it linger, time keeps moving on, and it is best that you keep moving with it.

Part of understanding that the past is in the past is to understand that you should not bring all of the negative thoughts and feelings and experiences from the past into the present. For instance, if you were the fat girl that did not get many dates in high school and college, however, you lost 75 pounds, you need to understand that you are no longer the fat chick and you should not let the hurts of the past limit your present and future.

One way to leave the past in the past is to understand that it does not change. Thus, there is no use in going over different scenarios of what ifs. If there is a different step or direction that you believe you should have gone in in the past, figure out how to go in that direction now. And if the door has closed on that opportunity in your life, find another door that you can open.

Change Yourself but Don't Try to Change Others

In life, we often want other people around us to change so much that we try to change them; however, this is far from a great tactic to us and often a waste of time, energy, and emotions.

If you want to see changes in your life you need to make them. Take active steps to make changes that will benefit you without expecting others to change with you. This is not to say that the people around you that you care about won't be willing to change for the better, but you to see let them make the decision that they need to change on their own.

And even if you can encourage some people to change, you can't change everybody, but you can change some of the people around you. Some people in your life are not going to be willing to change, and if they are bringing you down in any way, you need to get them out of your life. It is important to know when to cut some people out of your life who are treating you negatively or otherwise having a negative effect on your life instead of hoping and waiting for them to change.

Don't Waste Time on Envy and Jealousy

In life, we often look at others and wish we had what they have. Sometimes it seems as though life is unfair because we do not have those things. There is no usefulness in spending time thinking that things are unfair and being jealous of others. In fact, when others around you experience success, you should be happy for them and proud of them in order to be in a positive state of mind. Envy is a significant energy drainer. It is a lot more prudent to spend your time figuring out how you can better yourself than wishing you had what someone else has. If you spend your time thinking about how you can get where you want to be, you may even get what they have that you are jealous of!

Not Spending a Great Deal of Time Worrying About What Others Think About You

Spending time thinking about what others think about you is often in the same category as spending time thinking about things that you cannot control. It can be a major time waster.

Yes, you do need to care what other people think about you. You can't just ignore what other people think about you. In fact, if a significant number of people seem to be thinking the same thing, then they could be right. The world is full of other people, and it is better to have them on your side than against you and can make life significantly easier. You will learn more about this later in this book when you learn about emotional intelligence.

Be Thankful for Everything That You Have

People with mental strength garner some of it from being thankful for all that they have. This can especially to true in tough times. Instead of dwelling on the things that you do not have it is often better to focus on the things that you do. This can help you persevere and get through your obstacles and trying times.

Wallowing in self-pity, the opposite of being thankful for what you have is a habit that those who desire or possess mental toughness never display. This is an energy and emotion drainer that can keep you stuck where you are during troubled times, unable to move past them.

This is why you should count your blessings. During hard times or when you need some encouragement, you should even try making a list of the things in your life that you are thankful for. And everything on the list does not have to be something big. Look around at your surroundings and in your life and try to find some small things that you can be thankful for. Noticing all of the little things around you that you can be grateful for that you overlook on a daily basis can help you to understand how lucky and blessed you are and give you the strength and mental toughness to go on day to day and pursue your life's goals.

Don't Criticize

People who are mentally tough don't spend their time complaining about and criticizing situations around them. Instead, they look of the positive aspects of things instead of focusing on the negative.

Either find some way to change whatever it is that you see that's flawed or let it go. Complaining does nothing but causes you and the people around you to hear a bunch of negative thoughts. In fact, if you have a habit of complaining, you may develop the reputation of being a negative force of a downer to people that have to listen to it.

Live in the Present, Not the Future

The present is now. Many people are aware that it is damaging to spend a great deal of time living in the past; however, you may not be as aware that it is just as damaging to spend too much time 'in the future' as well. If there are things that you need to do to achieve your goal, a new goal that you would like to achieve, something that you would like to do, or even something as simple as making sure you do something fun that day, don't wait for a more convenient time in the future to start these things.

Not wanting to live in the future is especially important when it comes to enjoying your life. It is important to take some time out to have fun and enjoy life in order to stay mentally and emotionally balanced. Because everything in life does not always work out as planned and some goals that you set you may not end up achieving, one way to avoid becoming frustrated and lose your willpower and determination is to make sure that you do some of the fun things that you have been waiting until you have more money or until your kids go off to college to do.

Lesser scale traits of mental toughness.

There are some characteristics of mentally tough people that can be seen in some of the things that they do that may not, at first, be obvious to people who are looking on. These are smaller than the aforementioned traits and characteristics of mentally tough people, but they are still worth mentioning.

1) Mentally tough people also display the ability to forgive.

It takes a mentally strong person to forgive others for things that they have done to hurt them. Holding grudges is mentally and emotionally draining and can prevent you from partaking in some opportunities. However, it is important to examine why something happened to determine if it was a one-time thing or something that is a part of a person's character. This is because even though a mentally strong person has the capacity to forgive, you still should not let the same person burn you over and over. A mentally strong person also has the ability to recognize when someone needs to be eliminated from his or her life or at least kept at a distance. That being said, forgiveness is for the forgiver. It lets a weight off of your mind and gives you inner peace with regard to the situation that took place for which you are bestowing the forgiveness.

2) They ask for help when they need it.

A lot of people may be too proud to ask for help; however, mentally tough people are strong enough to ask people for assistance when they need it. Asking for help shows that you understand your limitations and you are willing to sacrifice a small bit of pride before you fail to do something properly.

3) People with mental strength are financially responsible.

It is important to be financially responsible so that you can save money for the future and afford the things that you need. It is also important not to overextend yourself credit wise so you can buy things such as house and cars and get school loans. Mentally tough people understand this and are willing to forgo some of the little things that they would have like to have in life now in order to save money and ensure that they have good credit. In fact, short of a tragedy, the overwhelming majority of people with mental toughness have good credit.

4) Mentally tough people manage time wisely.

Just as people with mental strength manage money wisely, they also manage time wisely. People with mental strength understand that utilizing their time wisely is important to being able to achieve all that they need to do throughout the day so that they get everything that they need to get accomplished done and turned in on time. This is a sign of maturity, something that responsible people do.

5) People with mental strength are humble.

Mental strength and humility go hand and hand. People with mental strength do not need to be arrogant about their accomplishments or toot their own horn. They feel that if they do a good enough job in work, school, or life, their work and accomplishments will speak for themselves, and they can carry themselves with humility. If you feel the need to be arrogant, ask yourself 'Where are you falling short that your work and life do not already speak volumes about where you are?' Realize. However, that humble is not the same as self-deprecating. Don't try to make yourself smaller to make others comfortable; but, be a big enough person not to brag.

6) Mentally strong people know how to pick their battles.

In life, there will be numerous times when you and other people tend to disagree. You do not always have to speak up and show it. Instead, it is often best to pick and choose when to speak up and when to let some things good for the sake of keeping things running smoothly and preserving amicable relationships. Although you should not shy away from conflict if it is necessary for you to stand up for yourself or some other important reason, you should not shy away from it either.

7) Mentally strong people realize that although they have control over their own lives, everything in life isn't fair and they should not expect it to be.

Yes, you should believe that you have control over your own life; however, it is unrealistic to believe that simply working hard, doing all the right things, and being a good person can get you everything. Some people are born with more, some people are given things, and some people are lucky enough to win the lottery. That's life. It does not make sense to spend time thinking about whether or not everything is fair. The answer is no but that you have to live with.

8) People with mental toughness treat others fairly. Treating other people fairly is a very important part of being a strong-minded person. We have all seen someone who appeared to be easy to take advantage of. And there are a number of people out there who certainly would do so. Getting something this way seems to be easy and fast, but it should also be against your morals and values.

This only gets you somewhere in the short term. It can damage your reputation and make you seem like an untrustworthy, scandalous, unreliable person who may take advantage of others. Even if the vulnerable person was the only person who you took advantage of, it is everyone would trust you less because of it. This is one thing that is not worth doing to yourself in the long run.

Chapter 3: Why Develop Mental Strength?

The answer to why develop your mental strength is a rather easy one – because if you have not taken the time to do it yet, there is a good chance that your mental strength is not as developed as it can be and you are not able to achieve your goals at the level that you would like as a result of this fact.

You should develop your mental strength so that you can be more productive in your life. Productivity and mental strength go hand and hand. It takes mental strength to concentrate on tasks and fortitude to finish them. This is especially true with complicated tasks. Productivity is one of the key factors that determine how well you perform on your job and in any other tasks that you choose to undertake in life. If you lack productivity, it may be due to lack of concentration, being distracted by your emotions, lack of drive, energy, desire, and more. To become more productive, have more success in your career and accomplish more of the things that you want to do in your life, you should practice mental strength exercises. You may even get that raise that you have wanted for so long!

You should develop your mental strength so that you can overcome challenges and hurdles. Mental strength gives you the ability to overcome challenges and hurdles. The difference between people who keep going when they reach obstacles that they need to overcome on their way to a goal and people who do not overcome these obstacles but instead turn away and decide that the tasks are too tough is that the first group possesses mental strength. Mental strength is what is needed to see a way around the hurdles that you face in life and try to go around them so that you can achieve larger goals. Thus, lacking mental strength allows you to only achieve smaller unimpeded gaols in life that are easy to attain.

If you ever desired to get a job which requires you to have a master's degree or a PhD, you can either see the hurdles ahead of you such as lack of time or lack of money or energy or you can see the opportunity for advancement in front of you and decide that these aforementioned hurdles can be surmounted. This is not to0 say that these hurdles are less real or apparent to the people with the mental strength to try to go past them and enroll in the school program that they want. This hurdles are just as real and may result in struggling and difficulty for a time; however, the people with mental strength are willing to handle these struggles in order to achieve the end goal whereas the people who lack mental strength try to avoid the struggles toward the gaol and thus avoid the goal itself.

You should develop your mental strength so that you feel that you have more control over your life. In order to have control over your life, you need to have mental strength. Mental strength conditions you to believe that you have the power to control the things that are going on around you.

You should develop your mental strength to adjust to change.

The world is changing everyday. Many so-called baby boomers know that when they first entered the workforce, it was far different than it is today. The use of computers was minimal, and the internet was not as popular as it is today. Social media was nonexistent. Then a change came that hit the workplace and society in general and these older members of society saw the skills that the younger generation possessed take over even after all of their years on their job and seniority. Some of these people may have had a hard time adjusting to the changes that were taking place; however, those who wanted to be successful worked hard to make sure that they could keep up with the changes that were taking place in society so that they could fit in with the times and still have value at work that would allow them to receive the salary that they desired and qualify for the jobs that they wanted. This is something that is normally discussed with the younger generation which is just coming in to work. Flexibility and the ability to adjust to change are keys to longevity that one must possess to keep going and stay current in this world. Mental strength allows a person to realize this and make the changes that he or she needs in spite of p0ride or years of doing things a certain way.

Change comes at many times in our lives. Sometimes change comes when you move to a different city for a new job. Sometimes change comes around when you leave a relationship that you have been in for a while such as what occurs with a divorce and sometimes change occurs when you enter a different stage in your life. Many people try to resist adjusting to the changes that are occurring and what things to stay the same. People with mental strength, however, are mentally tough enough to understand that changes take place in life and in order for you to be successful and live life to its fullest, you need to change with it.

To establish a winner's mind

Working on and establishing mental toughness is like setting a standard of excellence for yourself that causes you to strive for a higher level of excellence that you may have ordinarily strived for had you had you not worked to cultivate your mind. It is like setting a higher level of expectations for yourself, and you are aware of what these expectations are. Oftentimes, thinking that you can do or excel at something is half the battle and when trying to establish mental toughness, conditioning your mind for winning thoughts processes is very important. Your mindset can help you with your willpower, dedication, time management, and the other essential things that you need to do to establish your goals and to succeed at the things that you set out to do.

Mental toughness promotes longevity in your career or goals

Mental toughness is what allows you to stick around in your career or at your set goals. For instance, let's say that you want to be a dancer. You must undergo a great deal of practice and training to get started. Then you go on a number of auditions, a number of which will be rejections. You may hear criticism of your skills in a not so friendly manner, maybe even a little hurtful. If you ever want to get on Broadway, you have to go through all of this and that just to make it in the show. After that, there are rehearsals, shows, and more rehearsals and shows. If you do not have a strong mind, you are not going to make it that long under these conditions. It is very important that you use your mental strength to keep pushing on and to help you understand what you are working for.

Building mental toughness allows you to stand up for the difference between right and wrong when others won't

Most people know the difference between right and wrong, but does that mean that they are willing to stand up for it? It takes mental strength to stand up for what is right when other people won't. You may feel like you are standing by yourself which can make you nervous and a little scared but you will only be able to stand up for right versus wrong if you build up enough mental toughness to withstand the crap that gets thrown at you for not staying on the

side of the majority of the people.

Mental toughness allows you to be able to handle distractions and keep your focus.

Building mental toughness allows you to keep your focus and not be swayed by distractions when they come your way. This is very important because life is full of distractions and you will run into a large number of them if you want to achieve lofty goals. This distraction will not knock you off your game as much if you have a strong mind and the ability to focus.

There are a lot of things in life that may cause someone to lose their focus. Everything that happens in life generally involves some type of emotion and not having mental toughness can allow these emotions to take over your thoughts, cloud your judgment, cause you to dwell on issues instead of using your time wisely and be an all-around distraction. Even though you may have a number of important things to do, you will find them very difficult to get done if you cannot focus. This can even lead to dangerous situations if you become distracted while driving or doing other things that really require concentration.

Mental toughness is the answer to being distracted. Although mental toughness does not allow you to block out emotions and emotional situations, it does allow you to handle your emotions and emotional situations in the proper manner so that you can address these issues at the proper time and still be able to function during the day.

Mental toughness allows you to be able to prioritize.
The new slogan Priorities First is very important. You need to handle your priorities first and then handle the rest of the stuff later. It is not okay to neglect your priorities for something that seems more enjoyable or more important. This can cause you a great deal of problems in the future, and you will regret it. Mental toughness helps you understand your priorities and your obligations no matter how many other things you need to do.

In life, there will be a great number of things that you need to get done that may cause you to neglect your priorities. This is simply a fact a life that can not be changed, and you need to have the mental toughness to figure out what your priorities are and how to get everything else done without neglecting them.

Mental toughness helps you to identify and change irrational thoughts

Mental toughness allows a person to identify irrational thoughts so that you can address these thoughts and their origins and replace them with new beliefs that are more accurate. This is very important for people to do so that they have an accurate perception of the things going on around them. People who have not established mental toughness often stick to old belief; however, people who have developed mental toughness have the strength to examine their beliefs and admit when one of them falls short from what is rational and let it go. Establishing an accurate perception is very important because your perception is your reality. Inaccurate perceptions can skew your way of thinking so that you cannot make proper judgment decisions.

Mental toughness teaches you patience

You cannot have everything at once, and mental toughness will help you with patience in the same way that it helps with willpower. You cannot expect immediate results. Time and patience are part of the key to success in the long run. You can expect to get everything at one time; therefore, patience is a virtue that mental toughness instills in us.

Mental toughness gives you greater life satisfaction

Mental toughness helps to increase a person's life satisfaction. This is because it gives you the basic tools you need to succeed and the drive to do it. Mental strong people are able to handle life, in general, better than people who lack mental strength. They are able to control their emotions, work more efficiently, they are better listeners, and they bond better with others.

The people who are the most satisfied with their lives are the people who make wise choices and exercise some form of control over themselves. It is very important to control the need to spend money, waste time, or do harmful things that seem fun at the time. Developing mental toughness affords you the mental resources to live your life more responsibly. This is the primary reason that people who have taken the time to develop mental toughness are more satisfied with their lives.

The fact that someone has spent time honing their thoughts and brain power into a winner's brain also shows determination. This means that this person is willing to do what it takes to achieve his goal and one of which is life satisfaction. Mental toughness helps you understand that it does not make sense to complain that you are not satisfied with your life and not do anything about it. There is no point in expecting anything to change unless you take steps and do something to move toward happiness.

Mentally tough people plan out goals that are the steps that move them along the way to happiness. These people do not take no for an answer. They are strong enough to face challenges that they may encounter and determined enough to make it to the point at which they feel that they can rest assured and happy that they have done all that they could do to be satisfied with the way that their lives are going and the way that it turned out.

Mental toughness is akin to inner strength, and it makes life easier in general

Developing mental toughness does for the mind what working out does for the body. It makes your brain stronger, faster, and better than it would have been if you had not taken the time to do so. Thus, mental toughness is like a workout routine for the mind that strengthens your thought processes, your emotions, and your resolve to succeed.

Just as working out makes it easier for you to walk around, jog, run, walk upstairs and participate in daily activities, working out your mind by developing your mental strength makes it easier to think under pressure, establish and fulfill goal, focus on the things that are important at the time, establish willpower and more.

Many people do not have the mental strength to make tough choices and take the steps that they need to to get them done. This makes their lives more difficult, so it is very easy to see why mental toughness makes life easier. It is much better to be mentally tough, with inner strength, than to not develop your mind just like it is much better to be physically strong than it is not to develop your body because you never know when you are going to need to use your mental strength and fitness just like you never know when you are going to need to use your physical strength and fitness. But it definitely makes life easier to have it so that you never get caught off guard. It is of utmost importance to make sure that you mental toughness skills are at their peak when you need them so that you can navigate through the things that may trip others up in life and give them a difficult time.

Mental toughness allows you to reduce stress and anxiety

Stress and anxiety, a subject that will be discussed in more detail later in this book, are harmful to your mind and body if left unchecked and allowed to fester. Stress causes a number of health problems, both mental and physical. It can affect everything in your life as well. You may become agitated when you get stressed out and take it out on those around you including family members, children, co-workers, friends, strangers and more. This can cause problems in relationships that may be hard to fix if done repeatedly, over a period of time, or the stressful situation is not fixed.

Stress is not something that should not be addressed; however, people who do not have fully developed mental toughness skills may not know how to cope with stress healthily. They may come up with negative solutions to dealing with stress such as drinking, smoking, and more. When you develop your mental toughness, however, you develop skills to help you adequately cope with stress and stressful situations so that they do not get out of control and you can handle such incidents and occurrences better.

Furthermore, people who do not have mental toughness skills suffer from more stress than people who do. There are a number of reasons that stressful situations arise. One common reason that a stressful situation occurs due to poor time management. For example, let's say that you have a project that is due on the first of the month and you have had two weeks to complete it. You know that you should start on the project immediately, yet you choose to procrastinate until you only have four days left before the project is due. If you had managed your time properly, you would have had it completed with ease; however, because you failed to manage time properly, you are down to crunch time. This can cause you to stress out about whether you will get your project done in time. In addition, you may become stressed when thinking about whether you will be able to complete the rest of your obligations. If you had developed your mental toughness skills before this situation arose, you would have been less likely to fall victim to stress. This is because you would have understood the importance of managing your time properly and had the discipline to do so.

There are many other examples of how mental toughness skills and development can help you to reduce, avoid, or alleviate stressful situations. This is because mental toughness involves discipline and being disciplined in areas of your life helps to keep you from finding yourself in negative situations which can cater to the creation of stress and anxiety.

9 781801 676953